I, Ursu

RUTH STACEY

V.

Published in the United Kingdom in 2020
by V. Press,
10 Vernon Grove,
Droitwich,
Worcestershire,
WR9 9LQ.

ISBN: 978-1-9165052-7-8

Cover image: 'I, Ursula' © Magdalena Kaczan, 2020.

Cover design © Ruth Stacey, 2020.

Printed in the U.K. by Imprint Digital, Seychelles Farm, Upton Pyne, Exeter EX5
5HY, on recycled paper stock.

V.

"I love you to pieces, distraction, etc."

J.D. Salinger, *Franny and Zooey*

"Wulf, Wulf, it's waiting for you
that's making me ill; that you take so long coming
makes me pine away, not being hungry.
Eadwacer, can you hear me? A wolf
will carry our poor child off to the forest."

Translated from the Anglo-Saxon by Fiona Sampson
Folding the Real (Seren, 2001)

V.

For Lawrence, of course

V.

Contents

V.

V.

Averse Muse

If you don't want
poems written about
you, then

do not make me fall in love with you
by seducing me softly until the honey
suckles.

You should flee female poets; their call
will transform you into a buck
leaping to escape the word dogs.

This is solid advice; it is true.
Beware, your brown eyes will turn bitter –
I am not just this season, not your bit of fun

because I will write poems that will petrify
your royal jelly into wax; I will
describe the growl that you make as you come.

Rose Red

Bears are not good fuck buddies.
They get possessive. Casual is not
part of their lexicon, relying on growls,
gruff prose huffed into the neck.
You can hardly make out the words
because bears are distracting
when they are inside you.

They wait in woods,
in fact, any tree presents danger.
He will leap out, brush against
your thigh with such melting softness,
his brown eyes will beseech you:
fall with me.

It is not the claws that cause girls
to hesitate, mostly they sheath those,
except when the moment calls for slight
pain down the spine, the snarl of mine.
No, the things that make a woman pause
are the metaphors.

Every kiss is a parable – the glint of gold
beneath the pelt, the prince within
and the beast in the bed.
It gives me a headache; the worry
that the treasure he grinds for won't work,
the spell won't be broken this time.

It seems like we have never spoken,
only screwed till we ache and the pillow
has my face shape.
In fact, bears make lousy lovers:

they crap in corners and moult
so the hair gets everywhere.

He brings me white roses that smell
of other girls; it is torture.
The snow is melting and I throw him out
of the doorway, my foot in his ample arse.
I just can't stand him anymore.
I sweep every part of him away,

the tufts sparkle in the daylight.
But at night, as I brush my long dark hair,
plait it into ropes, I dwell on how
he would bite my cheek red,
and I hope he comes back.
I miss the warmth of the bear in my bed.

Decorative

A Golden Shovel using the Golden Rule of William Morris

There are colourless times when I consider what I have.
Strip back the illuminated walls and there is nothing
but plaster and dust, an illusion of decoration to dwell in.
Three players: a king, a queen, an errant knight. Your
design is a triangle, Arthurian, acted badly in these houses.
Before I realised, I stepped into a mimed role, one that
I could never change or alter. A part in a masque you
wanted to play out. Inevitable adultery. I decided to do
what I felt best; I am no legendary queen and will not
perform the script. What can I illustrate that you don't know
already about sorrow and longing? It is rose petals used to
make jam; the pale pink jelly is nothing like I want it to be.
Impossible to capture the smell or beauty, it is only useful
food rather than the ambrosia I imagined. Portrait or
photograph? In one I am a goddess, in the other I believe
I am myself: mournful, thoughtful, entirely Jane. I want to
transform myself into another life, one free of you, Will, be
far away from legends, imaginings and never, ever beautiful.

The Exchange

A simple thing; she needed a boy, I wanted
a girl so we swapped them, only a few hours
old – what did it matter, who sired them.
We laboured together, holding each other.
Friends, that's what we were. I had seen
his displeasure as she repeatedly failed
him and gave him daughters: five pale
chicks hatched and named after virtues.

I took her home, called her Dorothy.
My little doll, fists like clams.
Her elderberry hair still stuck
to her head with her mother's
blood. I held her to my breast
and she sucked; tender conspirator.
My husband was away and then
we were as unreal to him as soil
after wave, his feet could not get footing.
One morning he was gone, the smell
of sea salt still in the bed sheets.

I see her once in a while, the gaggle
of daughters behind her, husband striding
ahead in his Sunday clothes, carrying my boy
proudly on his shoulder – copper hair
catches the light as he marvels at clouds.
Dipping her head like a tulip, her
voice cautions the child to hold tight.
My hair smoulders; her parchment eyes
fear the heat. The Vicar talks of sin
yet the devil must be in me for
I care not. And still, the girl thrives.

Signals

Do reindeer hooves have sharp edges?
Crescent shaped through chipping
flakes away, hit gently with your hammer stone.

Flint-edged, so when they walk on shingle
sparks hiss with white-blue flares –

it sets the dry brash on fire,
roaring louder than this easterly wind
that whips my hair, or hers.

She is sat on the beast's pitched, stiff back
holding the leather bridle.

The silver of the deer's muzzle hair
matches her folded, embossed tunic.
We admire the photograph, her cool eyes.

I fan the smoke your way
but you refuse to read the shapes

as it curls and sinks and punctuates.
I am yours, you only have to look
at me, just a backward glance –

your arrow always hits the target,
a Parthian shot: you taught me that.
History gallops without stirrups

and in our bed I dress your dark skin
in borrowed clothing from the steppe.

Narrative

In the forest the brown-eyed man and grey-eyed woman make their way through the humped roots and duck their heads beneath the low, moss-covered branches. The woman is carrying a baby in her arms. She trapped the man by handing him the child; one confident embrace of the infant and he passed her audition for the role of father. Rescuing them from the darkness. He is happy! He never held a baby before. Love is exuded from the child like breath. Mayflower trees smell like flesh. They are a family in the woods. You imprisoned me, he will later say, it is your fault we have all these babies. Wanting to return again and again into your soft body. So many children; they follow the trail of cake crumbs. Her grandmother had cared for the man when he was a toddler in the nursery she worked at. You were always cold, she said, always wanted to be held. Then he left the Kingdom and lived far away, across the violent sea. Only to return and meet the woman. This kind of coincidence is storytelling at its best. Only his heartbeat causes her to relax like the mammal she is. They married in the little church with harvest vegetables watching the blessing. She misses her grandmother amongst the daffodils. Besides, he says, your eyes are blue.

Actions Speak

"Patience must be the charm
  To heal me of my woe"
Thomas Wyatt

Invitations to bed are soundless;
that moment on the moor, shrill wind
shushes and the trees pull their creaks
into their heartwood and watch
the rooks touch beaks on their branches.

Those invites laden with wetness,
caught in a sudden cloudburst,
goose skin and clinging gingham,
the second-hand copy of Wyatt's
poetry discarded on the picnic blanket.

Suggested with a glance and that subtle
change of expression, the invite
without words: flick of the lace fan,
a handful of flowers (roses of course)
always the rose red and red and bed.

You know the kind of invites I mean?
When the eyes become deeper pools
and you feel the slick pull,
the fascination that drowning holds,
seaweed wrapped around the legs

and the blackness coiled waiting
like a crumpled night sky
that reflects a cavernous sea,
lit only by those strange electric fish
and you say: *you talk too much*

and kiss me to stop the words that boil
from my tongue as I try to cling on

to everything; pinning moth-winged
letters down in my collection book.
Silently, you show me what is louder.

Extinction

Mermaids drown in fresh water,
the lack of brine causing them
to gum apart like paper dolls.
Yet the fish women persist
through the brackish waters,
searching for the hot-blooded
ape-men who walk on land.
Mermaids yearn for dry,
incandescent embraces.
So unlike solitary spawning,
watched but not touched
by stagnant, dank mermen.

River water eddies;
it is caressing the pearly
skinned, persuading them
to ignore the bitter sting.
Nervous flutter,
the elegant fingers flare
protesting disintegration.
Silver tails softly dissolve,
billows of carefully
combed hair drift away.
Scales float back
to the sea, returning
to the mermen
who see them and know
they are finished.

Camille Claudel

earth below and walls around me I am here I am here free Camille can you hear me only the cat listens and there is no respite from this despite to create I am still here clay soil slip plaster cast bronze swirl jealousy devotion unlock this cruel prison away from solitude creation crafty devil do not fear the letters burn one by one smoke rises there are two men outside the shutters clay clay clay bronze I sleep completely naked to fool myself into thinking you are here I cannot rest I wish to walk into the forest and set fire to the trees wax wax figures into the fire with you melt limbs and eye sockets into nothingness free this prisoner free wax bronze shapes fingers changing inanimate into life life strife free me I am me I am Camille

Lady of a Portrait

The trouble began when I told him that
from now on I would only wear tea gowns.
His shoulders set, he put down his knife
and stalked off to sulk in his growlery.
I cannot help it, I long for loose folds and drapery
that can move with my flesh,
rather than the constraint of the corset,
the binding weight of the bustle.
We argue in whispers of what gossip will come,
people will say his wife is lost in a widden-dream.
He touches the edge of the translucent fabric.
I know what he thinks;
only his eyes may look at my body
wrapped in fabric that light can seep through.
My mind weaves through the embrangle
of rules that demand I must be contained.
Brooding on the muliebrity of womanhood,
I remove my choker and throw it at him.

Ornamental Fabrics

Velvet

Bury me in velvet, the dying Queen ordered.
Perhaps the only thing luxurious enough
to rot at the same speed as royal flesh,
or maybe tenderness was what she desired
for the last act her body would perform.

Lace

A little noose, to ensnare the unwary.
Glimpsing flesh through a million tiny holes,
more enticing than bared skin. Cuffs,
necklines, hems; all the places where cloth
ends and the person's skin begins.

Waterhouse's Missing Painting of Danaë

Stolen from the home of Mrs Julia Ellsworth Ford in 1947,
only a black and white reproduction remains.

The box is cramped and utterly dark.
Waves are stilled; salt holds them.
The baby's fingers twine her hair.
He sucks her breasts dry and wails
for moisture. One gold coin falls.
She fumbles about the damp wood,
moves it up her thigh and stomach.
Places it into her mouth and sucks
the taste of the God from it; pollen
sweetness of blossom unfolding.
They wash onto an unknown shore;
the breaking lid lets the sun pierce
their eyes. Perseus is silenced.

The room is dark and entirely empty,
only the painting hung on the wall.
The collector is still; the canvas holds
them. Teal blue waves lap the shoreline.
Each pebble and rock glistens –
tender strokes of the painter's brush.
Lamps pinpoint the baby in her arms,
the set of her jaw as she protects him.
Golden box contained in an unknown
home; the sailors fall in shock, faced
with Danaë's beauty. The collector
thrills with keeping it secret – it turns
them on: their silent, selfish ownership.

Fox Boy: The baby with all the hair

The hospital lights are rushing
bright; smile cannot be unpicked from
her lips, the nurses coo to each other
and peep around the door,

Come and look!
Is this the baby with all the hair?
Oh, isn't he beautiful, look!
Look, at all his hair –
where is he from?

Here, he's from here.

In the street she carries him in
a striped sling, close to her heart –
she won't be apart from his wily
beats; people

jostle to look at his face
invade the space between mother
and child, she is kind though
and she doesn't mind them stroking
him, except when they say:

What is he?

A baby.

Fox Boy: Dewey Decimal

diversity
the tick box
this is no dewey
decimal, no sense
to this, putting people
in boxes

bark like good dog

veer between refusing
and trying to be helpful

should be an easy task
pen on paper
down stroke and up
best describes: no no no
none of those
mixed is their phrase

mixed, other

The Actress & the President

The suit jacket is shucked at the door
      beneath the woven fabric
            the silk holds his smell:

orange peel and deer musk.

Her grey fur coat abandoned
      on the wooden floorboards
           curls in submission.

      He will later claim she cast a spell.
      Such 17th Century fear
      of witchcraft   that says a woman's body
      must hold danger and entrapment.

She will murmur in her defense –
he always had the promise
of piled-up kindling in his eyes.

If he had paused in his antelope tangle-leg
struggle to leap into her embrace
      he may have realised his animal mind
was urging run
      run away
not because of her spells
or sharp teeth   it was his
      morals pricking
      at his thumbs.

Iseult Gonne

The thunderclap
did not come:
where, where, where

are the rolling clouds,
the slim streak
of white anger?

The wind roars
and disturbs the ears
of the queen.

The candle is lit
and blown out,
lit and blown out.

You cannot create a life
out of a dead baby –
you just can't do that.

Dance on the edge
of the ocean
but peace never comes.

Eyes are always
watching the shape
my shadow makes.

If you bruise and
confuse the leveret
the hare will flee.

Air

our house is yellow and it sits on the edge of the field with the main road ribboning the other side my father burnt his foot when he was four he put a kettle on the flagstone floor to make his mother a cup of tea he stepped in the boiling water his skin peeled off with his sock what did grandma say? he does not remember the dog kills a bird it is so light and warm the book says it is a thrush buffeted by wind on one side and the sound of cars approaching and leaving at a whoosh on the other but we don't notice the howls anymore the first time we made love I cried with joy is that important? you turn and call to me I will never know what you shouted the air dissolved it the baby walks along the hedge chattering reggae plays on the stereo in the car we share a pipe and don't speak just look at the view 54 46 that's his number everyone deserves to be free warm blood melts into something turn your lights down low the child asks me a question and points but I cannot understand him the wind absorbs all vowels the axe is moving the air as well fast and swift and splitting the logs two children swing back and forth the air moves with them and the girl's hair is long it whips like a horse's tail

Woodlander

A stillborn baby must be buried too;
any tree may mark the grave he thought best.
To not know makes any wooded view
a cold graveyard instead of a forest.
Things are not spoken of – they are dormant,
hidden with the little corpse in the roots.
Why do they persist to rustle and sing?
The song of the trees seems drowsy and blunt.
Endless falling leaves will burst from her shoots:
oaks would weep if they were remembering.

The trees do not hide from a blue-black kiss;
they do not recall the previous fall.
Leaves they have nurtured they will not miss,
forgetful as they obey nature's call.
How does he not make them tremble?
The trees have the gift to dismiss past pain,
sharp edge of axe they somehow suppress.
How I wish my thoughts would dissemble
like these verticals just aching for rain;
just branches and rings of forgetfulness.

Little Corpses

Never walk on a frozen lake.
It may appear as thick as your arm
but the silent water deceives with places
of thinness: beneath bridges and where trees
slant over, the eager crack and quick swallow –
no little corpses under the ice.

Never play on the railway lines.
Metal tracks shimmering into the distance
give off the image of adventure; they lie.
When your friends taunt you to follow them,
say nothing; march off with a strong spine –
no little corpses smashed by a train.

Never go off with a stranger.
If someone calls you over, walk away.
Push down your natural instinct to be polite.
Most people are kind, it is true, but some
monsters will look as human as you –
no little corpses hidden from view.

Dark Thoughts, Lately

I am afraid I may crack open
like a tree struck by lightning,
be nothing more than a husk
full of beetles and fungus.

Poke me with a willow stick
and my body would be dust.
Did anyone gather the ashes
of the Jacobean witch women?

Perhaps their children would
wait for the embers to cool
and fill a sack to take home,
embrace it during the bat-dark

night, when only the wolf
smiles and the rest of us shiver.
It is always the river, deep
and cold like the cruel slap

of the midwife after the heart-loud
clamour of the womb.
Do I long to return or escape –
the water is gloomy but peaceful.

Could I leave them without a body
to bury? O my little children,
could I leave you without my ashes
to hold in the middle of the night?

Fleeces

The conversation drips like laudanum
from a thick glass bottle;
they are sheep butting heads in a field
of grass comparison – who has the best grass?

Are our lambs at the right school
to get the high results to land
the correct job to buy the
most grass?

I just like to smoke grass.

The woman opposite me picks the poppy
seeds from her cake and licks the yellow
crumbs that are left; her tongue is grey.
The coffee is steaming.
If I don't leave soon, this will kill the ink
bird I keep in my underwear.

Instead I take the butter knife
and cut a diagonal slice from my stomach:
white rubber drips and collects in my lap.

I shape it into a bowl and fill it
with the brown sugar lumps from the heap
in the centre of the table.

The cotton tablecloth keeps trying to rise
up from the polished dark wood and become
a ghost, but I keep my fingers on it, firmly.

Gilt

1: adjective – covered thinly with gold leaf or gold paint.
2: noun – a young sow.

How can I help you? What do you lack
to be beautiful? Here all your dreams
can come true, just sign on the dotted line.

The Doctor will see you now; he can fix
each flaw and revamp the whole body,
transform you into a goddess.
So you can gaze down with your perfectly
sculpted breasts, six on each side of the rib
cage, descending in size like the flowers
on a foxglove. Anyone who is anyone
knows that two areolas are so out of date.

And your colour is not right, you must rub
yourself with bleach until you are sow-
white and then we will spray you each week
the exact and correct shade of gold;
it tells your audience you are perfect.

The Doctor's price? What is wealth compared
to holding your head up: beg, borrow, steal,
just make sure you sign here. The corn hangs
heavy in the fields waiting to be cut
and your new face is waiting to be cut.

Why are you afraid of the mirror? Pull
in your stomach. Pose. Open your mouth wide.
Wider: as if you were holding an apple.

Mental Health Animals

Between us, your depression and my anxiety;
such slippery things to articulate – yet I try.

You, a creature sat curled into himself, naked,
muscled, not a weak man but a hare-man.
Arms folded, long ears and face drooped:
blocking out everyone, but especially

me – a woman whose anxiety is a white horse,
pale in a dark green field. It is a pastel-soft
night, I am wearing a cherry-red dress, bare
footed – my uneasy horse is outside myself,

body trembling as there are no stars visible.
The heart cries: where are the Plough
and the Pleiades? I hold her muzzle close
to my cheek to calm her – don't pant so,

don't pant, my dear one. Your hare doesn't
notice my withers flickering or hear
my breath come like gasps of steam
in the cold dark air that surrounds us both.

Lazy-Pacing Clouds

The field is unseen, beyond our view.
Clouds have fallen low, low.
We force our clumsy,
thick-socked feet into boots
and part the air like a curtain.
Stepping on to the stage, the thrum
of the earth mimics the clapping
beat-beat of an audience.

This is the slow, slow time.
Above us, nothing but grey drapes.
The water in the air cups our faces
and smooths from chin to brow,
like an eager beautician applying
storm-scented creams. We have no
words, just shiver-stumble after the dog.
Our rented cottage crumbles behind us.

Living here is living with the sky.
See it, coyly threaded with white ribbons.
Peach-ripe and lavender-tinted at dusk.
Menacing, whale-heavy, dark and ready
to burst. Or this, near and intimate,
wanting to touch the people, trees and soil.

Pay attention to me,
the low clouds gargle, hear
my rain-full soliloquy.

Haunting Dante

Do you believe in ghosts?
That they wait for a loved one to follow them?
I could tell you of burnt women who wait
for their children, slim logs turned ashen.
Singed pamphlets spiral like leaves.
They wait with me, words like white swans
that die, and their mate is still living;
they wait with me. I can hear them all.

Their necks are translucent like silken screens,
purposeful puppets dance on sticks.
Hats bend our necks, wide-brimmed like Saturn.
Paper poems held in the arms as currency
with soil to hold one in place.

The racket of spades. To be disturbed,
dug up, the words stolen from my resting place.
Words as nebulous as stars, the plum-cheeked
flesh is cold, unheated by a single candle.
My soul dissolves and I am free of him.

The Civil Wars of the Crows

Parliamentarians
they endure

no King Rook to lord
over them   each caw
and croak equal
to the next   so guttural
conversation floats
on the wind
as their stick nests sway and bend

a magpie delights
in taunting
them with her Old Birdish
chatter at the base of their tree

her avian profanity
slices the air like a sword
through flesh

   curse you c c c curse you all

the rooks discuss
higher things in the cloud wisps

the gaudiness of the monochrome
one is ignored

she shrieks louder
Cavalier blue flashes
on her black feathers

they fly higher

circling and   calling out
to one another
I am here
      I am here   here

The Poisonous Tree

The yew tree is cut down and a curse takes hold:
ripe as a fat yellow plum it weeps sickly juice
as the flesh begins to mould; the curate sickens
with a cancer deep in his spine, the cows break
the fence and graze on the humps of corpses –
the old woman had warned no good would come
of it, no good would come; *you reap what you*
sow, Solomon Hodgkiss, she muttered but he lifted
the axe and felled it anyway, orders are orders
and now he is dead; his baby born in the Autumn
storm has one blue eye and one green, *mongrel*
they whisper as she walks by; the spire still
reaches for the sky and the man who lodges with
the Widow Sanders grows his beard to his waist
and mutters words that sound like lamentations;
he grabs the smallest of the farm boys and pulls
him to his cheek and growls something about
self-chosen sorrows pain men the most but the lad
twists in his grip, snaps out an oath and limps home
to his mother before he hears the rest, yet he often thinks
of those words later, when his hair is grey and bitter
silence fills the corners of his house, spaces he
cannot heap with his regrets, they refuse to solidify
and that was long ago; the yew tree grows again –
a small tree but relentless and stubborn with berries.

Jeanne Hébuterne

I paint quickly, staring into a mirror propped
against new canvases.

Modi sketches me; my neck slicks into a snake.
Brown eyes tender in his version of my face.

Peach and pink oil paint on my skin:
painted becomes my skin.

My brush echoes the blue of my robes
in my cheekbones.

Auburn hair held back by a circlet of fabric
transforms into a headdress.

Queen-fierce expression stares out,
reflected from my mirror into portrait.

He lowers his sketch of me to note
I capture my soul more accurately than he.

Discovering Emilie Flöge

Those long-limbed, sinuous-necked women
in Klimt's paintings, drowning in golden fabric,
sirens and goddesses, decorative as peacocks.
I thought it was all his imagination. The invention
of the artist: the mosaic-gilded medley of shapes,
loose sleeves hanging with folds. All his; flicks
of oil paint invented and applied with a knife.

Black and white cloth, stripes, swirls of colour.
But no, he was painting from life. She designed
the clothes, and he embellished them. Men do.
She squints from behind him, next to him: sepia
prints do not capture her full couture rebellion.
He did, and now I view the women in his work
with a different eye, unveiled, costumed by her.

Exit Songs

The last thing was something solid, immovable,
an edifice to attach dead flowers to.

What interests me are the songs playing when they
checked out. I wonder: did the radio cut out?

Or did they hear a last vivid second of song?
What was playing? You cannot say.

But I pray, let it be you tuned into Radio 3.
An accident, a stumble through the channels –

porcelain thin, an aria smoked. Some opera singer
lifting her voice to see you on your way,

and not that when the door clunked open and you
were absent in the eyes

of the paramedic, sighs echoed from Radio 4.
But perhaps it was just silence, your bloody silence.

Vorspiel

There is an angry beast in the house. Hide, children. Stay quiet. Come into my arms and listen to my raised heart-beat. Da Dum. Da Dum. Keep quiet and stay out of the way. Chords in E♭, bassoons and horns, the rising arpeggio and the strings represent the river, the forward flow of life itself. Eggshells are underneath your feet. Children, listen, he loves you really. He is very, very ill. Words are inadequate salves. Little eggs everywhere. Quiet. Shhhh. Crunches echo. Membranes are thin. Glue won't set. Tape flutters off useless. There is a ringing silence. The beast is a soft loving bear. Tears roll down all our fur. The mirror smashes, bad luck. Glass so tiny when broken it becomes glitter in the currents of air. Radiant. The beast is gone and the man thinks he may as well be dead to protect us from the sadness. There is no fear like opening a door to find your lover swinging. My heart is a hare released to run this way and that, but there is no escape. He won't do it, he promised, but he may be persuaded. The irrational may seem rational, in a flash. The instruments all expel sound in a crescendo and the opera begins – what went before, what inspired it? The imagined therapist is French, with tender hazel eyes. Tell me the context of your pain? Une absence. Who left you? Mon père, mon père, mon père. A new world, an old world, which? Puis, s'il choisit la mort, laissez-moi au moins le trouver et pas les enfants.

Fox Boy: Answers

The small boy hunkered down,
grabbed the fox by the leg
and dragged him from his earth,
blinking and growling.

Fox shook his head, licked his fur
back into place. So?

Boy sat in the dust and bit his finger
nails to the quick, I want to know.

Fox stops chewing on an old rabbit skull
and looks at him. Do you look like a fox?

Yes. The child pulls a strand of his copper
hair and holds it in the light.

Then you are a fox.

But I look like a man too.

Then you are a man.

This is confusing, the boy sighs.

No, it's simple.

Fox Boy: Earth

They are hiding in a tree,
a yew thick with old needles,
red berries that stick to the skin –

it is only the fox and him,
looking down with clear eyes
at the dead and living bumping
into one another, fighting
about the belonging name.

Fox growls, it's only a word,
an idea, besides we were both born
here, from this brown earth.

Boy thinks – a naked fall
into stinging nettles, then

he says, but my grandmother came
from far away, across the sea,
does she belong?

Fox smiles a toothy grin,
Does she want to?

Not Letting Go

You have your back pressed
against a doorway full
of those twisted creatures;
I know the ones –
all teeth and selfish cruelty.

Sometimes they leave you,
sometimes they bite your skin.

And that god-awful mist,
the stuff that is not a bit blue
but indigo, chill mud dredged
from the lonely depths
of your ocean. I know it too.

My back is also
turned against a doorway:

it is rough timber
hewn from the forest
where the roots of trees weep,
or perhaps it is gingerbread;
I do not turn to find out.

Instead we clasp hands,
the way people do who fall

from planes, facing each other,
even as the doorways call,
beckon us to turn and enter:
come they cajole us, *come back.*
Relax – our grip is firm.

Go Round

The dog is pulling my arm and you, child, pull
the other, dawdling and then you say
that the copse is a graveyard
for witches and each tree is actually
a stick and far above on each one,
there is a carousel horse that I cannot see.

That night the trees form a circle.
I cannot leave the round path, I weave
through the fairground horses stroking
the gloss paint. Each steed is hollow;
inside are the swathes of a
witch's long hair, still burning.
I wind the russet tresses around my fingers
and wrists like copper question marks.
The trees in this copse are slender;
they bend, swaying. The floor
is moss-strewn, a bed.
It is saying,
             this is not frightening. Witch grave
by a gate and this horse is fresh, the paint
on the fingertips tacky. The deciduous
trees are gilded with decay, framing the view
through the copse and beyond the gate.
It is a cut cornfield. Dull yellow stems
made vivid by an utterly grey sky above and a woman
who hurries across the scene pulled by a springing dog.
Droplets of rain hit the blue plastic coat of her child,
a child she turns to encourage along,
a child who ignores her and tarries.

On the Cautious Road

The hitchhiker holds his sign hopefully.
It is such a sad little sign,
limp and with a spelling mistake.
Yet it's the way I am going.
If this were 1943 I would stop.
If I were a man I would stop.
Why is he standing there, they ask.
I answer. My children look at me and say
Well, we could give him a lift?
I can't admit that I imagine the worst
that could happen, the things
they don't know about yet;
rare and unlikely but possible
chance of him snuffing out our lights,
their miniature bones lost in the earth.

So I quickly reply that this car is too
noisy for that traveller;
he looks like he has a headache.
We drive straight past.
The children wave.

The Curiosity of Redness

Peel a human and they are red inside:
the skin is a thin covering, shades
of brown from light yellow to warm
umber but they can all be distilled
to crimson, scarlet, vermillion, rose.
I know this as we have taken many
of the ape-like creatures and stripped
them down to the bones; ground them
to dust to try and understand the hate
and tender love they vacillate between.

We have no feelings, only curiosity;
that is the word humans use – I have
read their dictionaries and oil paint
charts, pondered on their destruction
and pointless cycles of war: it all
comes back to redness.

A blood womb delivers each one –
ruby-splayed bodies, the surprising cut.
Veins pour dark red onto tarmac
or sand. I observe their relentless desire
to disassemble one another... and yet
I must try to understand earthlings.
Understanding comes with replicating.
Their hunger for all this red, to spill
and get right down to the burgundy flesh.

Greenland Sharks

Samsara: the next body is determined by the state of mind at death

gluttony find wretched line flaw collecting done spittle dreams
filled skin sack slaughter home terrified sawing dark skies
flee look dulls flogs off land comet debris insidious thresh
caw fed sings see hell love causes heeds spit
lack doubt internal voice pit come me church
salacious brine hunger again ran ordeal occurs
foul release feasting thief dark caustic tide
ground scare he son-daughter dismal price
toward doorways shush dark

Forward, always, the shark.
Down where the salt water is almost ice,
bowels of the beast, teeth-sharp toxic hide.
Voracious canine runners, men in seal furs
hack out a circle and hoist it from the search
for dead things; the smell of corpses leads it.
The hook pulls: dogs cough and vomit the bilious flesh.
Chilled in black water, alone, parasites gnawing shark eyes.
Agony, blind – stretched time for reflecting on little screams.

Halfway Between Sadness and Distress

I am in the ocean holding a bird,
waiting to release it.
Waiting to let it go and find
my way to land

and to you.

You, who told me to stop saluting
those damn magpies,
those damn magpies that singularly
frightened me,

all feathers and beaks.

Black and white birds
that clenched my heart,
clenched my heart with fear that the luck
would run out

and it would be like before.

Only your strong shoulders
and fearless smile,
your fearless smile that dismissed
superstition;

you laughed at it,

made me bold enough
to keep my fist,
keep my fist in my lap
and not salute the little fuckers.

Smokes

I have no playmate.
I'm skittish as a gazelle.

You are a long way off
          roaming the savannah.

Come, sink your teeth into my shoulder

haul me up the tree and hang me
from a branch
dead weight for your next meal
licked   limbs sodden

cougar, panther: but lions
          can't climb high, can they?

So be my South American big cat:
slim jaguar with black circles
brown fur, brown all the way

bite, rip my pelt, open up

                    my rib cage
          white, brittle lines on red

and feast on my soft organs –
do they taste of grass?

Come with Me

After, sloth-like with satisfaction,
bed covers on the floor and panting,
we smile and ask: where were you?

Versailles: gold bedposts with raspberry
corset and cloud-white stocking ruffles,
you were a rakish courtier – and you?

Victorian attic: iron bed frame,
eager water flicking the window pane,
you were the sharp-eyed maid – and you?

Yurt: thick with clinging incense, the sound
of ponies stamping, bows and arrows,
you were a bold fierce warrior – and you?

Japanese garden: bright running stream,
maple leaves falling, painted skin,
you were the Geisha kneeling – and you?

Mountain air: fir trees and snow peaks,
creak of leather boots and eagle shriek,
you the lone-wolf in a cabin – and you?

Two Blades of Grass

What is unfaithful? A kiss on the cheek is not, when
done in passing, brushed and dismissed
like the previous century's fashion.

Yet, not touching but surreptitiously letting the lens
of the eye focus and dilate on his form across the room,
aware of him so skin feels the shade,

the imagined shape of fingertips stroking each ear lobe,
instep, ribcage, Oh! – then the blades of the shoulders
lengthen into flaming pale feathers.

Black-hearted desire is felt in the smallest of places.
It is white foam on wave swell, snowfall that eradicates
all sound, even the poet speaking. That is betrayal.

Distance

For Lucy Hewitt

I had rich friends before, but you were a different breed:
elegant, made of finer stuff than me, your body held
like a glasshouse orchid whilst mine was a hedgerow weed.
You caused a sensation, every boy at college felled
by the swing of your long hair and exotic expensive
otherness: they flocked and pestered you, compelled
like stupid bees drawn to a heady flower; I defensive
and jealous, why – because I wanted that attention?
Or now, as I look back, nostalgic and pensive,
I wanted you myself: your pollen-sultry adoration.
Captivated. Hearing your different politics, the violence
of our arguments, the passion: such a rich accumulation.
Remember that morning when we woke up late? Silence
outside the window, the white clouds had fallen low
and the moment was held in a calm, tremulous balance
and you so pretty in the numb, new, quiet world of snow:
I didn't want to go home, I didn't want to leave you and go.

Mute

Seven swans hook their necks
into silent question marks.

Why is the water just there
but unreachable?

Is this a punishment for the vain
and beautiful?

Waddling on a frozen lake –
the crust of ice denying

their elegance.
Sunrise, a church bell parts the fog.

The swans wait in humble
shapes for the first crack.

Infiltration

Get used to her calling him by the wrong
name, don't look up in puzzlement but smile,
say yes or no, answer her. Wear the mask.
Easy to get close to her, the attraction is real
not feigned: he wants to screw that body.
He whispers all the right things in her ear.
So trusting, never imagining he is reporting
back on a weekly basis, all the information
he gets from her. Names, dates of meetings.
He wears a long black coat and vintage hat.
Attends spoken word nights and broods.
Gets up and reads long lists of things with
the right amount of resentment for authority.
He listens to her whisper rhyming couplets
in her scented sleep. He feels some remorse.
The boss is pleased with him, says he is the
best undercover guy on the force. We'll bust
these poetry rings right apart by Christmas.
No more damn triolet codes to try and crack.
        No more subversive haiku
protesting government policies.
No more poets.

"A creature soft as snow, but with teeth of steel"

Prettiest of children: Angelica.
Framed, still like fruit placed just so.
Peach, pink, lavender, rose, blue.
Posed, wrapped in exotic silks,
those big expressive eyes that look
so melancholy. Petted for your pelt.
Russian princess, Sasha, white fox:
your sharp teeth will bite through myth.

        Why is the tawny bird in the room?
        It is banging against the window pane,
        Virginia tries, but she cannot catch it.

My fingers snatch but refuse to tighten,
making capture impossible, light
brown feathers masking the brittle bones,
and a solid core beyond my grasp.

Foolish Dog of the South

there was a time of endless days of frigid air and nothing to do
but mate and feast on geese, seashore scraps, slow
penguins that tasted of full and deep sleep
watch the violent sea ebb and flow

burrowed in ground as hard as teeth, claw, bones bleached
to reflect the multitude of white points scattered
across the darkness above, the yellow orb's
light was all that mattered

to the only ones on the islands who made milk for their young
tiny muzzles nudging each other away from the teats
each pale tawny and silken, warm blood
a clamour of beats

that was before the ship came and then everything was altered
one was taken and disappeared into the hull, his shade
returned, lapped by waves that sang of his leap
his choice to fade

onto the beach and into the all of their dreams, more will come
he howled in silence but they heard him and licked their skin
spoke their secret name to one another
said *this soil is made of our kin*

they appeared to the men who came to have no fear, foolish dogs
who came into their hands lured by meat, fingers skilled
at twisting throats to receive the sharp blade
so easy to kill

it unsettled the men, why did these dogs come into the tents, bound
up to them? at first they drew back at the perceived ferocity
until they recognised it was something else, they

called it curiosity

given a name, pinned down and categorised by the bearded naturalist
Canis antarcticus, a fox-like wolf, it didn't hold his attention
he shook his head and predicted it would finish like
the dodo, natural selection

if they were curious it was only to look closely at their destroyers
stare death in the eye fearlessly, for they were a brave tribe
who took their real name into the earth and folded it
back into the atoms, a human scribe

made a note, last Falkland Fox killed in 1876 to protect the livestock
the man who slit her throat would be haunted by the knowing
blackness of her eyes, there would be a reaping for the blood
he shed: man's bitter sowing

Muses

Calliope

Come, join my story as my heroine battles a dragon for the soul of her lost child. Listen, I will describe the many threads that lead to this outcome. I am the redolent reeds that grow along the banks of rivers, rotting slightly in the heat. Small fishes dart in the shallow edges of this place, can you catch one? No, try harder. The fire you try to stoke is full of wet sticks. It will never burn.

Terpsichore

The stage is dark when the orchestra begins to play; immediately engaging so that you are forward in your seat, eager to see the entrance of the dancer. Light hits her tutu as she bounds across the stage. It is a tulip bent heavy in the field. How they gamble on them. Bulbs of wealth. The wind catches the frills, orange, purple, pink and white. Rows and rows of them, in the orchard. A kite pulling on a string. Horses galloping across a landscape, jumping, playing: only they hear the music and the notes are promissory.

Following the Thread

You are stood in the walled garden,
trapped, caught on camera.
You are poised, waiting to be kissed,
shoulders tense against the warm bricks.
The leaves and roses hum with life.
Sticky webs enfold you and hold you tight.

Who are you looking at?
The handsome woodcutter who tells you
to smile? He came to rescue you from
the gossamer room you lived in.
Where you kept quiet, cowed by
those who begged you not to marry,

not to waste their hard-grown blood,
dilute them away to a whisper.
How you longed for him though,
until you became liquid,
hankered for the children he would give you.
Little fly who broke free from their web,

only to land in a stickier substance,
harder to disentangle yourself,
caught by the silken strands of baby hair.
In this photograph there is laughter in your eyes.
Your dark hair is soft around your face
like cobwebs.

Bikkja

It was imperceptible at first,
the slight lengthening of teeth,

then a pelt of hair grew shielding her legs,
catkins of fur hung under her armpits.

An unknown thicket he had never known
or explored appeared between her legs.

Where was the smooth dune of sand
he once skimmed his fingers over?

Every question answered with a growl,
each dinner put down with a bark.

At night he kept his eyes locked shut
as he listened to her curse and howl.

He used a silver spade to plant the birch tree

The vowels disappear from the conversation apart from 'I'.
Fade me out, he says, but the birch in the garden will know
how I was once here, my shovel in the ground, digging
the hole to place the tree in, how I knew your darkness.
Trees cannot remember anything but the leaves falling.
She adjusts her hair in a way familiar and annoying.
All the things here sound like insects' legs rubbing.
I am no longer myself and I have a lover; did you know?
A French king's infant son was thrown from a window –
it was the nursemaid, a game, thrown to her paramour,
the baby a ball: uncaught. Why the sudden scowl, my
once-love? Do you not enjoy the facts I summon, the great
distraction. Listen: the birch twigs are at the window –
if we carry salt into the garden, I can kill it at the root.

Inside the Riad

Apricot is the colour
of a setting ball of
flame, my beloved,
and the fruit
can be tasted this way:
follow the wet footprints
on the tiles, they spell out
your name –
come, ignore
the barred windows;
if you choose to leave me,
I will let you jump.

Fox Boy: Reynard

life hurts him in this skin,
neither reynard nor human

guile and blending in
foxed by russet hairs
that grow before the day
is done, the iris so brown
it shouts black: all faces sway
to them, curious…where
are you

from the slink of his hips,
the cut of the shoulders –
women pant and cannot put
their finger on

him, but they want him
surefooted, nimble, resourceful,
a survivor, shrewd, slippery
the best of both

oath: spat from a distance, folded
arms, that syrup silent menace

focused on his
sharp teeth; those canines that give
him away, gritted to ignore

the sound of hooves and hounds
baying

Fox Boy: Slyboots

hey you there slyboots

red-haired
dog, fuchs, fuck
you

zorro your name
slips from our tongues

liška, like milk,

hitting out as if playing
with conkers,
stamping down on you

as if on brittle leaves and not
your pelt, sionnach
smashing your skull

bloody skin
we have no thought at all
dumb rage

and still you laugh and bark
at the moon in the hope it is waning

ha ha ha haaa

Domesticated dogs can still howl but wolves cannot bark

The wolf comes to the edge of the yard.
I bark and he ignores me, stares
and stares.

We smell each other on the wind that blows
chill through the sap-filled trees.
My human

sits inside staring at the box on the wall.
She does not taste his reek in the air:
oblivious.

I know she cannot smell him or she
would be pressed against the fence
panting, like me.

I, Ursula

You tell me that still pools of water
used to echo the dead; I stare –
it reflects an ancient forest.
Spoor of wild cat, spoor of bear –
then a wind skims the surface

and the vision's lost. Tonight
you hold my body in the blackness,
huff into my neck and claw gently
at my flesh. There are symbols
in the weather that say yes.

Deep in the soil there must be
the bones of bears lying in the shapes
of forgotten landscapes –
the dark dream we wake up from
that was wild and unfathomable.

The Tonic of Wildness

I want to live somewhere wooded, so shade
is an everyday thing;
lead me through dappled places
where the trees rustle as the wind passes through.

Let's build our house out of logs you fell
so the sap can sink slowly through the walls.
I want to get up early, before the sun or children,
and glimpse a bear in the gap between
our world and hers.

Oh, you are good with engines and wires;
you could capture the sun and wind –
enough to spin an old record on the nights
I want you to hold me in front of the ash fire.

We could talk as we gather food,
smoke fish, pickle vegetables for the winter.
See the jars lined up on the back of the shelf:
jewels throbbing with preserved vitamins.

Retreat is our kind of survival,
even if it all has to crash, disintegrate and burn
for us to grow enough forest to hide in.
Keep your pockets full of acorns;
bury them in all the dirt you see.

V.

V.

V.

Notes and Acknowledgements

With thanks to the publishers and editors of the following books, journals and websites where versions of some of these poems were first published: 'Actions Speak' in *Hwaet!* (Bloodaxe Ledbury anthology); 'Bikkja'in *Abridged magazine 0-29 Primal*; 'Come With Me' in *Slightly Erotic Poetry* (Emma Press); *Distance* in *The New Humanist*; 'On the Cautious Road' on *Ink, Sweat & Tears* and in *Writing Motherhood* (Seren) anthology; 'In-between Sadness and Despair' in *Abridged magazine 0-34 In Blue*; 'Go Round' in *Goblin Fruit*; 'Signals' in *Brittle Star Magazine*; 'I, Ursula' in *Under the Radar*; 'Mental Health Animals' and 'Little Corpses' on *Ink, Sweat and Tears*; 'Gilt' in Envoi; 'Season Finale' in *Prole*; 'The Tonic of Wildness', 'Woodlander' and 'Domesticated dogs can still howl but wolves cannot bark' in La Questione Romantica; 'Fox Boy' poems from a sequence titled *Fox Boy* (Dancing Girl Press, 2014).

Thank you to all my friends and family who have read these poems over the years and offered feedback or encouragement. I am grateful to Luke Kennard, Carolyn Jess-Cooke, Fiona Sampson, Magdalena Kaczan and Sarah Leavesley. A special thank you to Isabel Galleymore for giving me feedback when I most needed it. Finally, thanks to the BB190 poetry crew!

'Decorative' is a golden shovel after William Morris' advice published in *Hopes and Fears for Art: Five Lectures Delivered in Birmingham, London, and Nottingham, 1878 - 1881* (1882).

'The Exchange' was shortlisted in the Plough Prize 2016.

'Camille Claudel' is inspired by Claudel's own letters.

'Lazy-Pacing Clouds': the title comes from Romeo and Juliet by William Shakespeare.

'Fox Boy' poems were inspired by the writing of Louise Erdrich, Gerald Vizenor, Thomas King and Linda Hogan.

'The Poisonous Tree' misquotes Sophocles.

'A creature soft as snow, but with teeth of steel': the title is a quote from *Orlando* by Virginia Woolf.

'The Tonic of Wildness': the title comes from a quote by Thoreau, from his book *Walden*.

V.

Ruth Stacey is a lecturer in Creative Writing at the University of Worcester. Her poetry collection *Queen, Jewel, Mistress* was published by Eyewear Publishing, 2015, and her pamphlets include *Inheritance* (Mothers Milk Books, 2017). A duet with another poet, Katy Wareham Morris, this explores 19th century experience of motherhood, contrasted with a 21st century mother's voice. *Inheritance* won Best Collaborative Work at the 2018 Saboteur Awards. A poetic memoir, *How to Wear Grunge*, was published by The Knives, Forks and Spoons Press in 2018 and was shortlisted for best pamphlet at the Saboteur Awards 2019. She is currently writing an imagined memoir in poetry of the tarot artist Pamela Colman Smith, as part of her PhD study.

V.